Elvis Darko's
56 billion dollar tour with Buffett

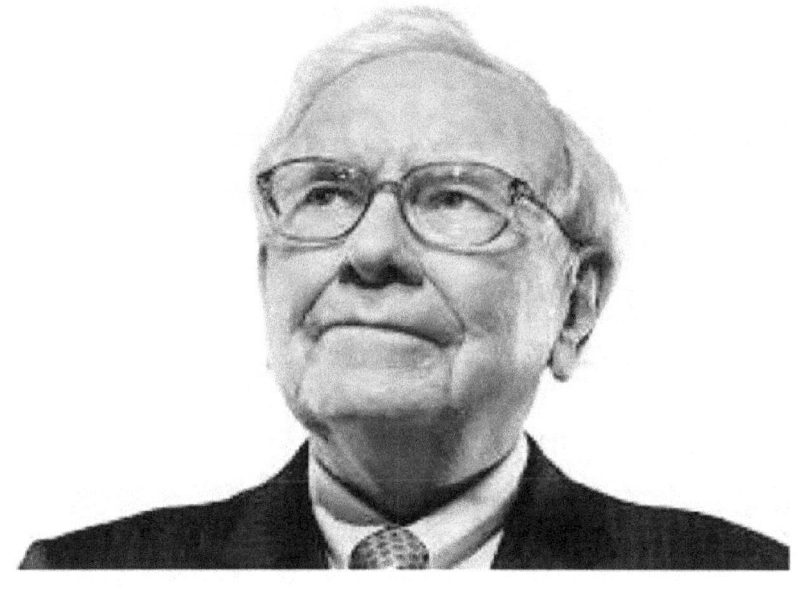

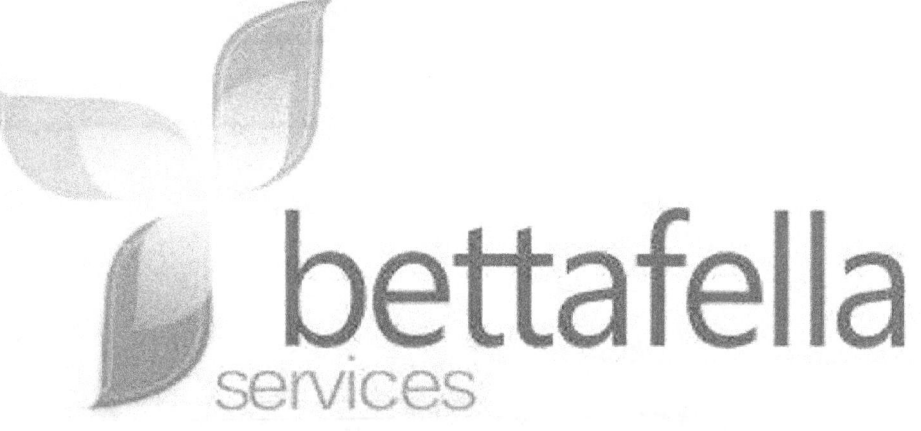

My 56 billion dollar tour with Warren Buffet

Elvis Darko

Elvis Darko

Copyright © 2017 Bettafella Entertainment

ISBN-13: 978-1547218530
ISBN-10: 1547218533

My mind and skills has been robbed so it is hard for me to express myself artiscally. I am lacking my styles and skills. I know English but I lost my English and knowledge after the robbery. So therefore I chose to make this work a short book. It is not even written in a proper book form but it is still fun and amusing

You will discover some of the greatest inventions you never thought i existed in this work and you will also get to know Mr Buffett dreams and real religious beliefs.

My books are coming out next year and I will tell you about them in this .

A portrait of Elvis Darko.

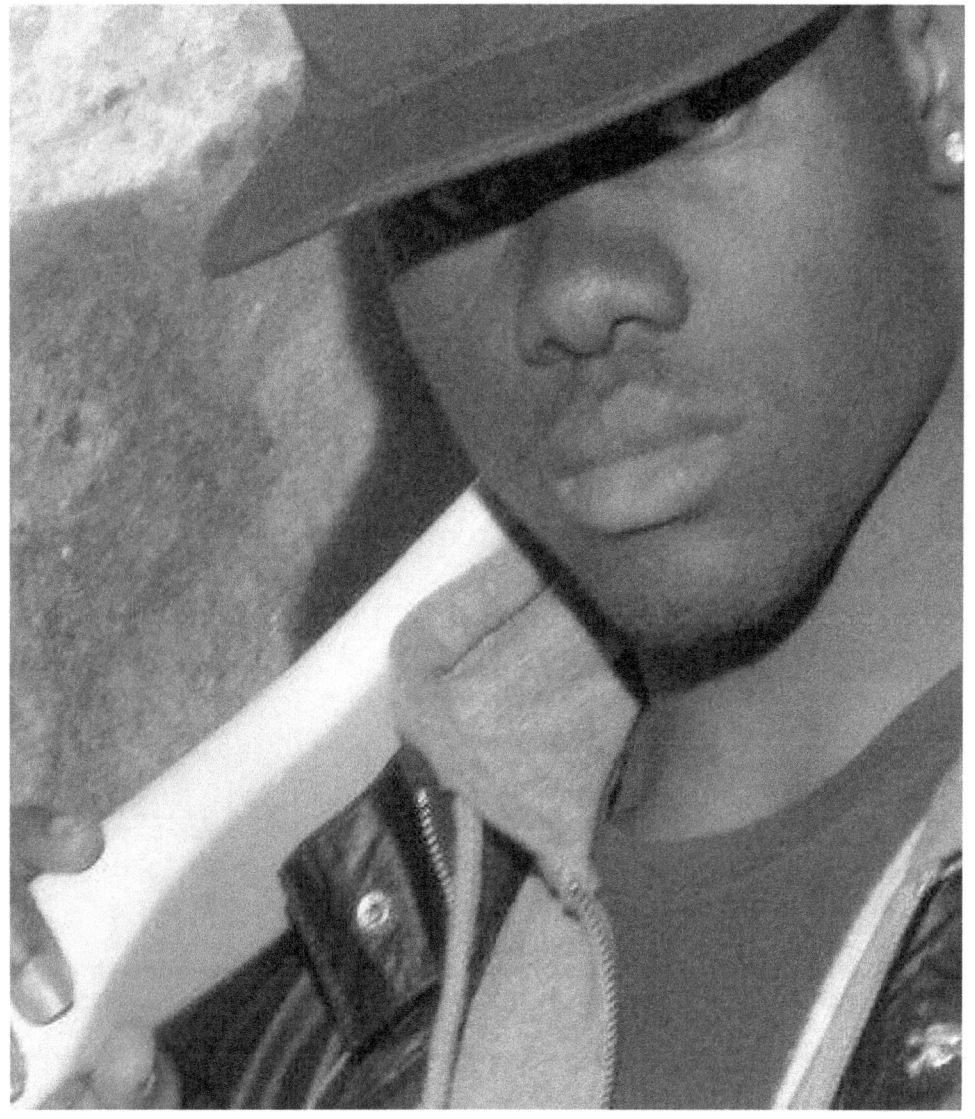

DEDICATIONS

This book is dedicated to Mr Warren Buffett r a strong sense of humour and the 56 billion dollar project.

To Mr Charlie T Munger for his advices and wisdoms,

To Mr Bill Gates who made my meetings possible. I thank him for the business ideas and advices he gave me.

To Mr Sean Corey Carter and his wife Beyoncé Knowles who made it work. Their support and guidance made it possible for me to meet all these wonderful people in the world. I thank him,

I love Music.

To Mr Ted Turner for his support.

I thank the Bettafella Team and everybody I worked with for helping me to accomplish my mission. I am on top of the world.

I love you.

ACKNOWLEDGMENTS

To GOD

I had a vision at 20 and this vision transformed my life. I shared the vision with Hollywood film makers such as Will Smith, Sylvester Stallone, Jay Z, Beyoncé and many other stars and we interpreted the dream very well. We had different interpretations of the vision.

We made music and movies with the ideas.

Here is the vision

"It was raining in hell.

The rain transformed into giant white male as soon it touched the fire. The man walked out of the fire towards my direction.

He was wearing a gold and white robe and his muscles were toned. He looked like a roman soldier from the BC.

His long caligae was the size of the buildings in the town. He was huge and he is the prettiest man in the world.

I was a 1 year old toddler in the vision and I stood in front of 4 brown souls who bowed and worshipped the white man.

The white male smiled at me and became happier after walking pass me.

I was only a year old so I was able to take one footstep towards the direction the giant white male went".

End of the vision

Get my book call the creation to find out the interpretation of the vision.

The Creation will make you stand out the crowd as an entrepreneur. It will make you an icon, a mega star and something of a phenomenon. Whether is a small company or a global corporation, The Creation will teach how to build and run a successful global business.

The creation will teach about how to succeed in your life. It tells its readers to chase their dreams to gain a better knowledge and understanding about themselves. Get it after the summer

.

"An autobiography of the richest African in Sweden.

THE CREATION OF BETTAFELLA.

by Elvis Darko

Introduction

I made myself a promise at 20 to make at least 50 billion dollar before I retire

I began to work towards that goal until I found out the meaning of what the 50 billion dollars and Manhattan, New York City really meant.

I got the chance to mingle with business tycoons, entertainers and global leaders after my graduation. I was an entrepreneur in the beginning. I retired and became a businessman and I retired as a businessman to be an architect and an Investor. Bad Boy's boss, Sean "Puffy" Combs called me one of the best hustlers in the world after I merged with Jay Z aka Sean Carter.

I met Mr Warren Buffett and he made a little tour called the 56 billion dollar tour to give us a better understanding of finance and what my 56 billion dollar idea meant.

So therefore I call this short work "My 56 billion dollar tour with Buffett"

I began my life as a professional entrepreneur and a diversified investor at 23. I invested in many different companies (lines) but music was one of my lines that blossomed. Music took me to the top of the world and saved my life.

When I decided to invest in music, I chose to do it in Ghana because it was cheaper to be a record producer. I invested in Ghana and we enjoyed enormous success in world with Azonto and Afro beat

My hustle contributed a lot to my success. I am an accomplished entrepreneur, titan and one of the best investors in the world now.

After my graduation, I spent time with Geffen Boss Jimmy Iovine, Aftermath's boss Dr Dre, P Diddy, Jay Z, Kung Carl XVI, Bill Gates, Mark Zuckerberg, Sylvester Stallone, Cameron Diaz, Kung Carl XVI, Princess Victoria, Princess Madeline, Beyoncé, Prince Carl Philip, Princess Sophia Queen Silvia of Sweden, Will Smith, Jaden Smith, President Trump, ex president Barack Obama, AL haji John Dramani Mahama, Aliko Dangote and Hollywood superstars.

My major breakthrough came when I made the decision to expand my business in New York and Sweden. Music executive and label owner is one of the coolest position to fulfil at the age of 20. I have gained a lot of accolades and titles but music executive is my favourite.

Girls who worked at the hotel that I stayed in usually wonder how I got so lucky and started my own company. It wasn't successful at first but I made it work. Business has never been a cash cow. I had other menial ways to make it work.

Jay Z, Nas, 50 Cent and all the hip hop heavyweights showed love and support.

After a successful trial with these music buddies, Mr Sean Corey Carter offered me and a distribution deal and I got the chance to mingle with some of his buddies. Cash Money, Bad Boy have also showed me love and support.

Bill Gates and Warren Buffett gave me accolalades nd we got the chance to talk about business. Mr Gates wanted manucfacture my own cell phones and my own cars. He calls t rich and probably I reminded him of Henry Ford.

My meetings with Berkshire boss Buffett lasted briefly. It was mainly about God and business. His money and financial secrets, he said he will let me know when we meet again. We also had discussion about the Almighty God and Jesus. He is a christian

And then I got the chance to speak with the Berkshire boss. I was starting up a global company at 26 and he loved our new invention call the "in". The " in" is like a different world or gaming world which turns your thoughts into a movie and virtual reality universe. You get to navigate through your mind and body easily with "in" technology .

I got that idea by chance and I am very lucky. I have shown this invention to his Hines Kung Carl, Bill Gates, Mr Sean Corey, Beyoncé, Ted Turner, Mr Trump, Aliko Dangote, Mahama, Simon Cowell, Jimmy Iovine, Mark Zuckerberg, Obama and it became successful.

The "in" can also help us predict what is going to happen in the future. You can also build and run your industry somewhere before bringing to avoid failures and defeats

Mr Warren Buffett had few inventions he wanted to develop. He wants to be able to bring his own private jet into somebody else's private jet and have a meeting.

He also explained how it would be easier to travel to a different country within few seconds with his other inventions and calculations . And then we completed the 56 billion journey.

It was very special and an honour for me to have met with Mr Buffett the Omaha oracle and the greatest investors in the world. I accomplished and gained a lot.

There will be a lot for us to discuss next time and I will record that in another book.

Thank you.

My other books, "How I raised trillions of dollars" and "How I turned 200kr to 30 billion" will be released next year 2018.

The creation will be out after the summer.

Thank you.

"How i turned 200 into 30 billion" is one of best money making book of all time.

It is a business and finance book that will teach you the principles and rules of wealth building and money making.

"Elvis Darko is a world best investor"- Warren Buffett &
Sean "Diddy" Combs
"Elvis Darko is the richest black in Europe" - Victoria,
Crown Princess of Sweden,

HOW I TURNED 200 SEK TO 30 BILLION SEK IN 4 YEARS

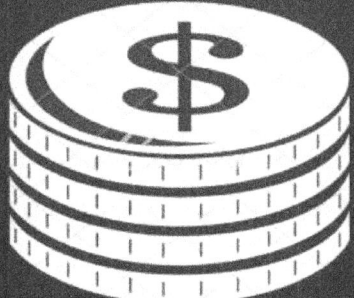

ELVIS DARKO

A book that will teach you the principles and rules of
wealth building and money making.

"How I raised trillions " is a best book in money making and building companionship.

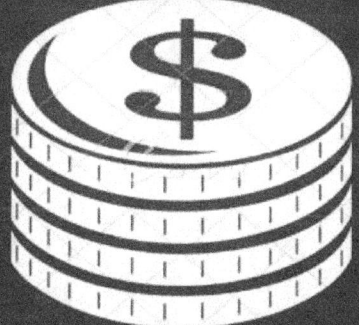

I will teach you about how I raised trillions of $ in this book. It will be released next year.

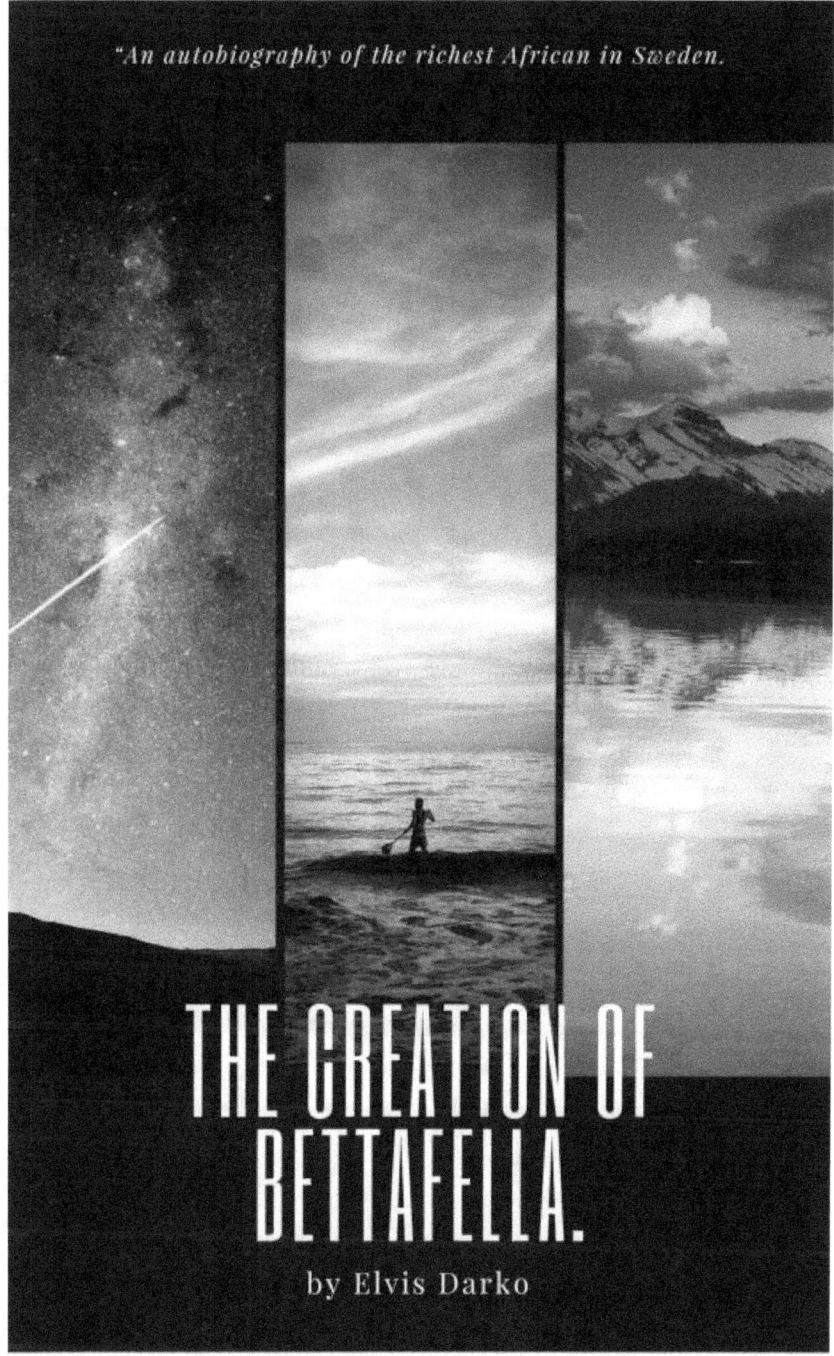

"An autobiography of the richest African in Sweden.

THE CREATION OF BETTAFELLA.

by Elvis Darko

END OF THIS BOOK

ABOUT THE AUTHOR

Bettafella

Elvis Darko born on, 11 05 1986, in Bomaa, Brong-Ahafo Region in Ghana is a Ghanaian and Swedish, accomplished entrepreneur, investor, music executive, titan and an author.

He is passionate about music and its role in the society and our lives. He sponsored, invested and produced some of the finest Afro-beats tracks in Ghana and Africa and has already enjoyed enormous success in the world with Azonto and Afropop

He has work with artist such as Sarkodie, Beyonce, Jay Z, Rihanna, Nas, kanye West, Madonna, Kelly Rowland, Will Smith and Puff Daddy and many more. Puff Daddy says he is one of the best investors in the world

He was Inspirational in the building and creation of TIDAL, a subscription-based music streaming service, which has an estimated net worth of 3 billion dollars.

He is also a great researcher who has carried out few researches with Microsoft founder Bill Gates, Warren Buffett, President Barack Obama, Michelle Obama, the Swedish Royal family and his wife Michelle Obama.

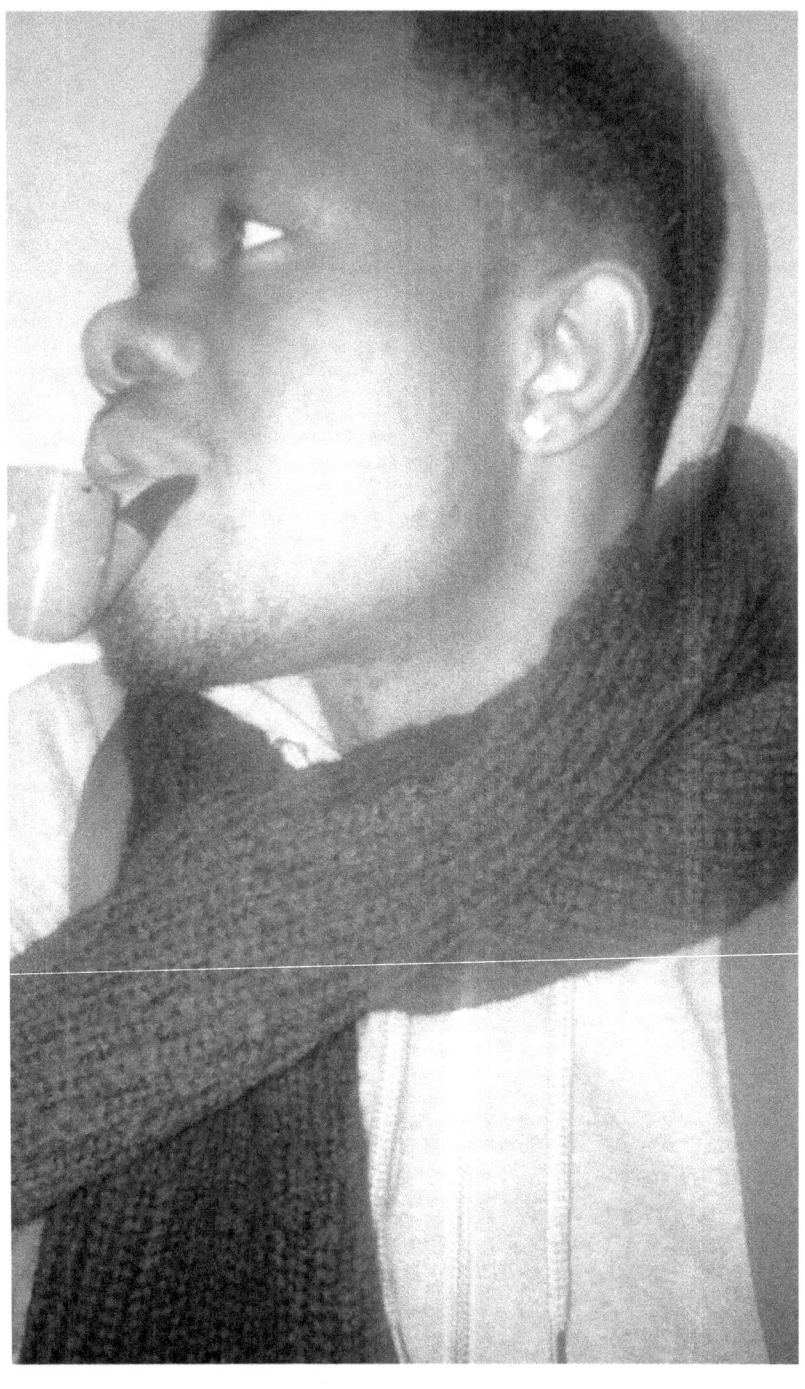

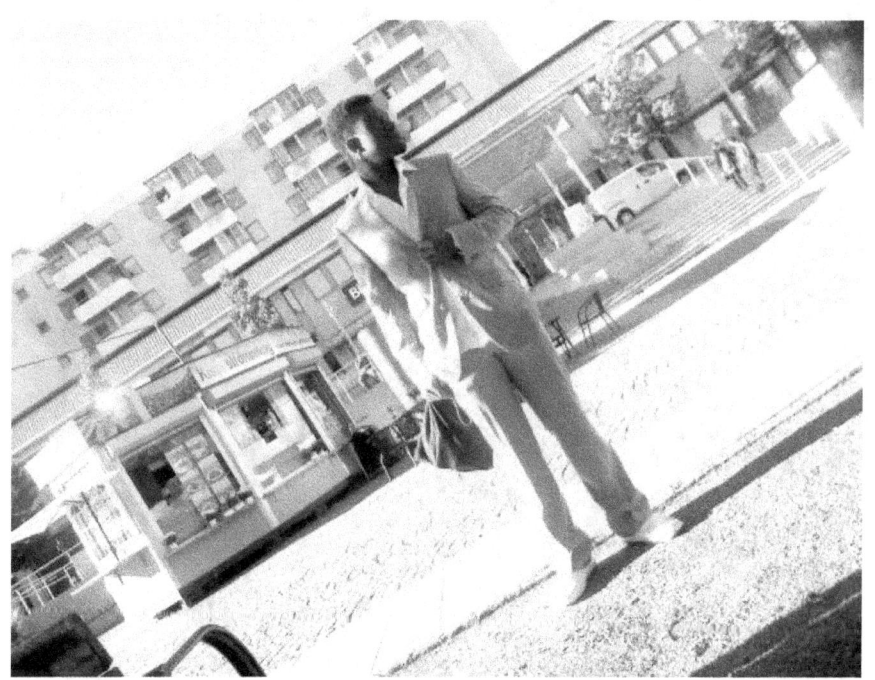

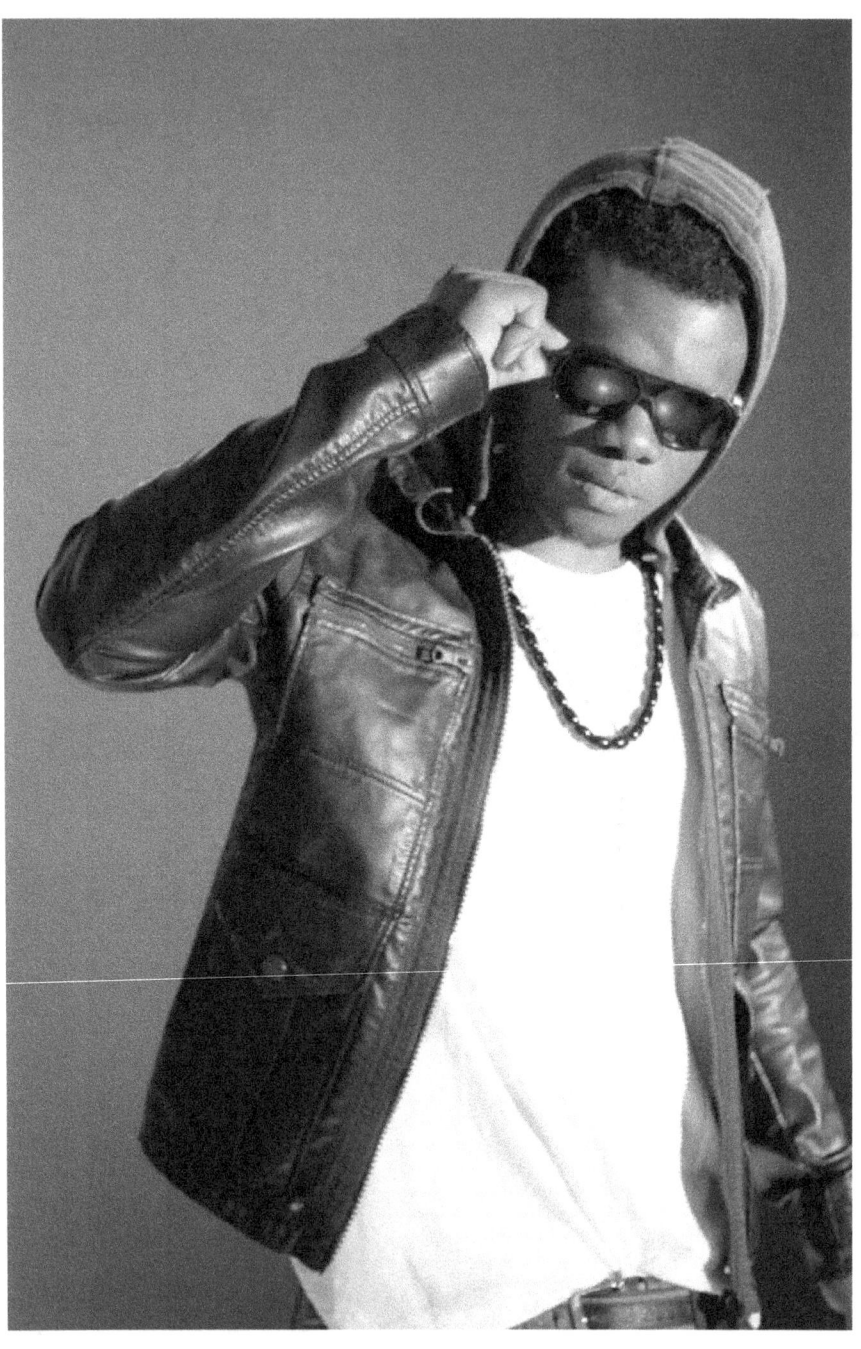

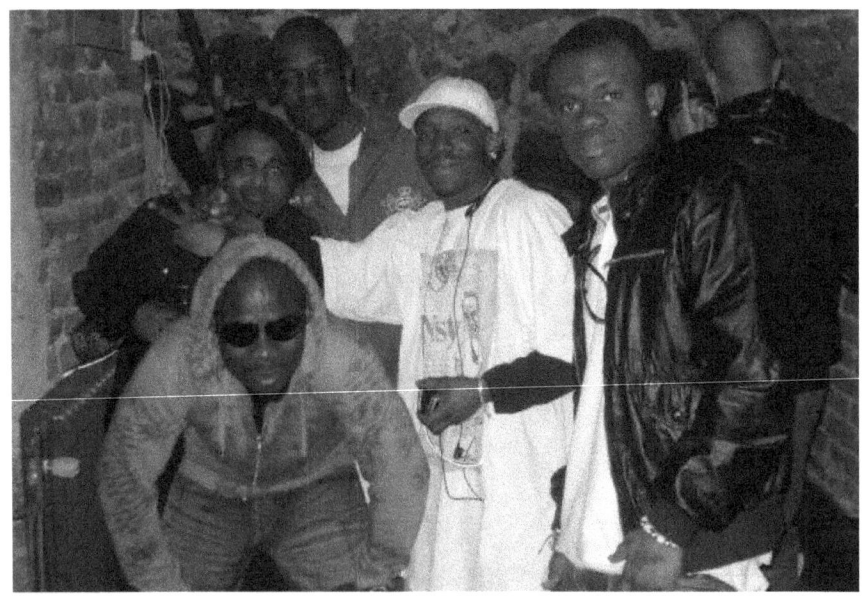

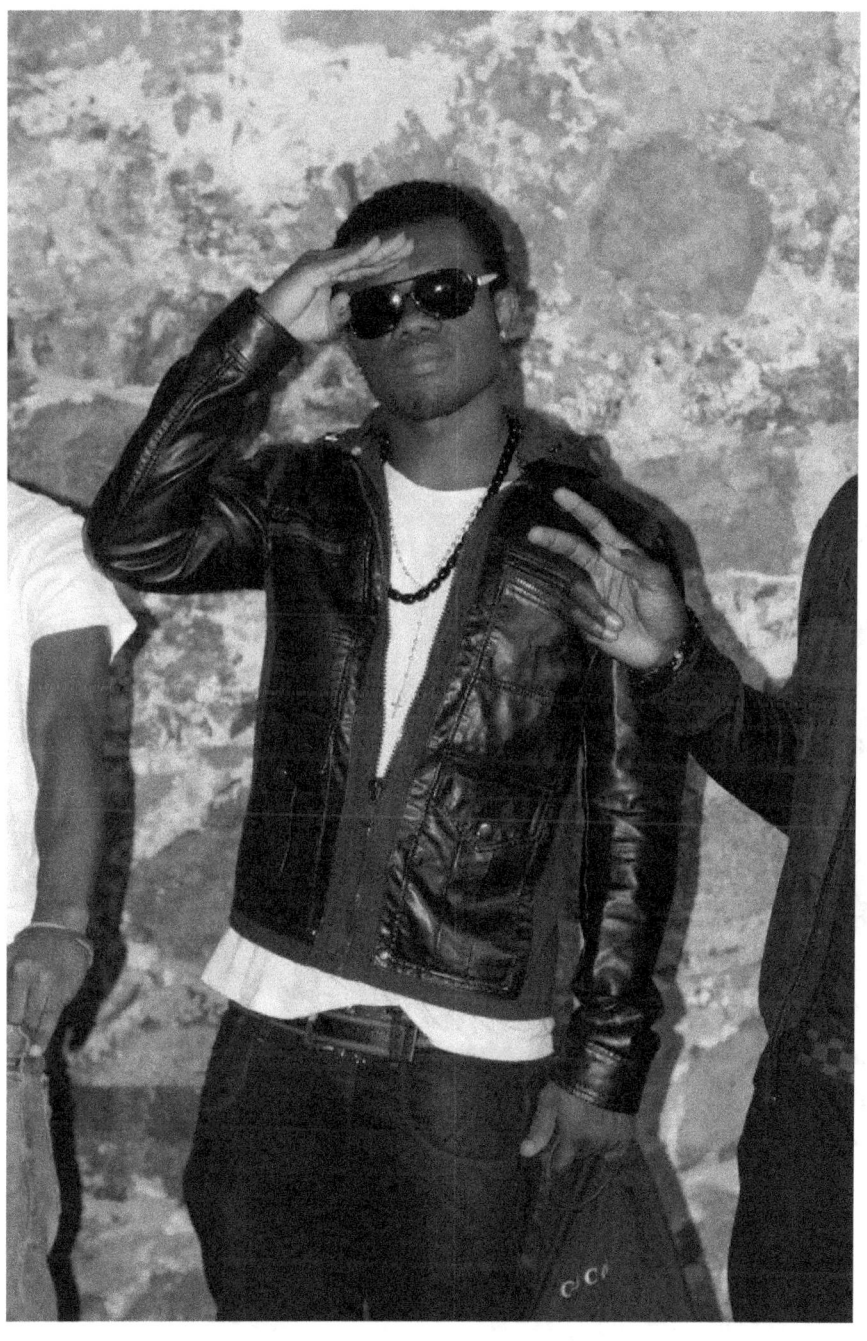

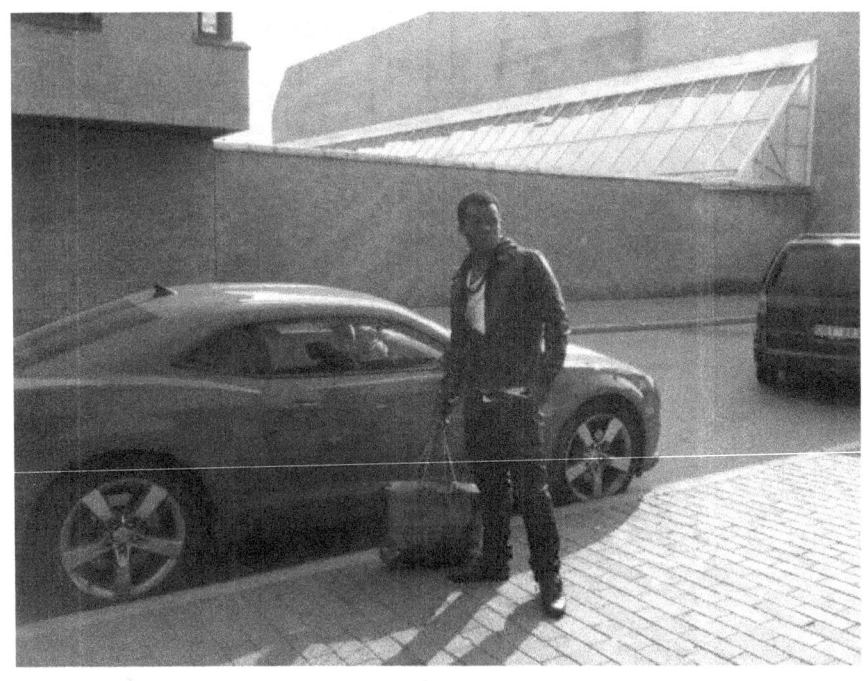

Jnjnj;oj v

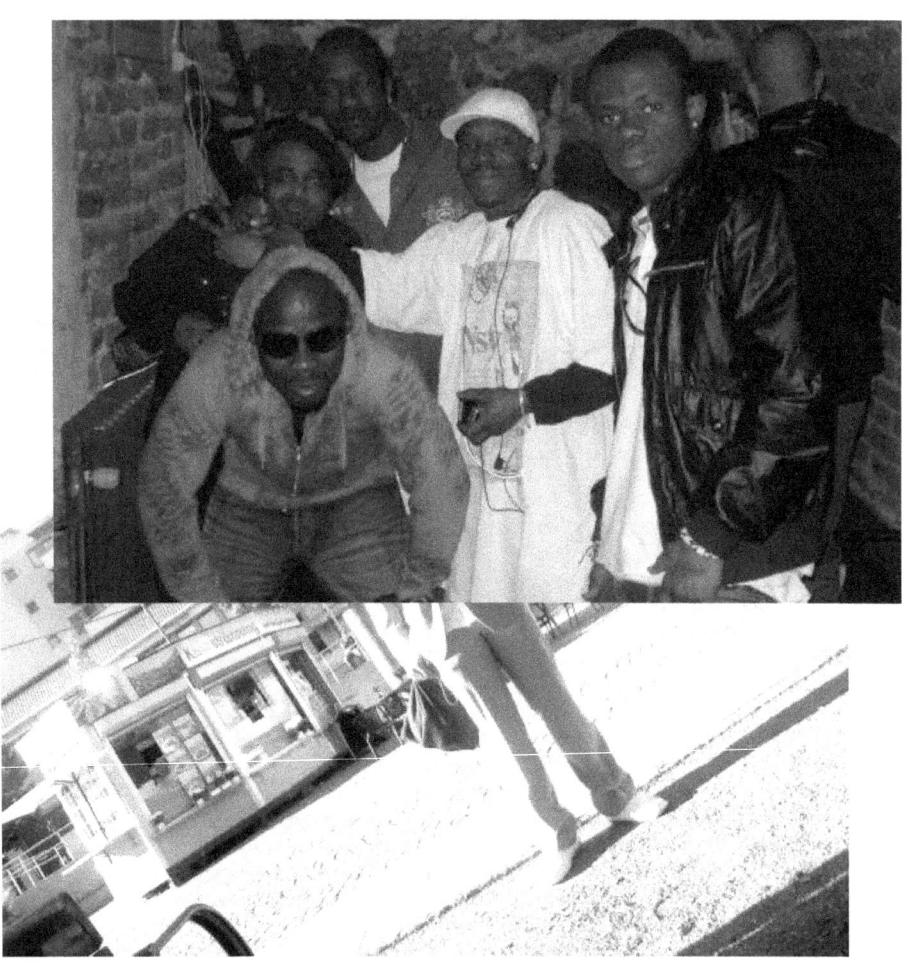

www.ingramcontent.com/pod-product-compliance
Lightning Source LLC
Chambersburg PA
CBHW072046190526
45165CB00018B/1912